SIDDUR KATAN LEADER'S GUIDE

Shabbat Prayer Book for Families with Young Children
A Component of the Minyan Katan Shabbat Service

by
Jaime Lewis
with Michelle V. Katz

Editorial Consultant:
Rabbi Lauren Kurland

ISBN: 978-0-87441-914-6
©2013 by KidsCan Music LLC
Design: Annemarie Redmond
Project Editor: Terry S. Kaye
Manufactured in the United States of America

www.behrmanhouse.com

CONTENTS

INTRODUCTORY NOTES 5
- Getting Started 5
- Notes on the Leader's Guide 5
- Room Setup 6
- Noise 7
- Storybooks 7
- Kiddush 7

SHABBAT SERVICE 8
Welcome: Songs and Introduction 8
- Shabbat Shalom 8
- Shabbat Songs (choose one) 8
  - "It's Shabbat" 8
  - "It's Time to Make the Challah" 9
  - "You'll Never Guess" 10
Introductory Remarks 11
Morning Prayers 12
- Modeh/Modah Ani 12
- Mah Tovu 13
- Hal'lu 14
- Bar'chu 16
- Or Chadash 18
- Sh'ma 19
- Mi Chamochah 21
- Amidah 22
- Oseh Shalom 24
Torah Service: Prayers, Activities, and Songs 25
- Vay'hi Binso'a Ha'aron 26
- "Torah Tzivah Lanu Moshe" 26
- Torah Time (stories, games, and songs) 28
- Eitz Chayim Hi 32
Concluding Prayers and Songs 33
- Ein Keiloheinu 33
- Aleinu 34
- Final Prayer/Song (choose one) 35
  - Adon Olam 35
  - "3 Stars in the Sky" 36
  - "Hamavdil" 38
Kiddush Blessings 39
- Before drinking grape juice 39
- Before eating challah 39
- Before eating cookies or sweets 39

INTRODUCTORY NOTES

Welcome to the *Siddur Katan* Shabbat Service Leader's Guide.

This Leader's Guide is designed to be used with *Siddur Katan* to create a spiritually engaging Shabbat morning service for families with young children. The service is targeted to meet the interests and needs of children ages two to six with integrated prayer, song, dance, Shabbat-related activities, and story time. Parents or caregivers participate in the service alongside their children, infusing quality family time into the richness of Shabbat.

This guide takes you step by step through the service with suggested talking points, detailed scripting, Hebrew prayers with English transliteration, English summaries of prayers, lyrics for Shabbat songs, family activities, and icons noting prayer and dance choreography.

Other components in the Minyan Katan Shabbat Service are: *Siddur Katan*, *Siddur Katan* Song Collection, and Torah Time activity inserts—all available at www.behrmanhouse.com.

GETTING STARTED

Begin by reading through these introductory pages. Then, move on to reading the service content sections as often as necessary to become comfortable with them. Your strong familiarity with the structure of the service and the script will make your Shabbat morning service one that engages and inspires families—and makes them want to return.

Prior to the first service, we advise that you meet with your synagogue clergy to confirm that you are following the prayer practices used in the main prayer service at your synagogue. If there is more than one children's service leader, mark which practices to follow directly in this Leader's Guide so all leaders can be aware of them. Additionally, work with your synagogue's administrative staff to ensure that the children's service has appropriate ritual objects, such as a real or plush Torah (or, if available, many plush Torahs, so that each child has a chance to hold one during the Torah Service), an Aron (ark) or a table with a *tallit* to cover the Torah, sufficient copies of *Siddur Katan* for all participants, and appropriate seating for participants (see "Room Setup" on page 6).

NOTES ON THE LEADER'S GUIDE

This guide is intended to be useful to leaders who have various levels of experience leading Shabbat children's services. It contains talking points (bolded on the left side of each page) as well as a full script (on the right side of each page marked with a megaphone). The prayers and songs, with transliterations, English summaries, as well as choreography where appropriate, are contained in boxes throughout the Leader's Guide. Note that italicized sections are for your information and are not intended to be read aloud. These sections are either notes to the leader or alternative activities .

Each prayer in this service is introduced with a "Simple Transition." In addition, many of the prayers have one or two "Expanded Explanations." Use the "Simple Transition" to tell participants which prayer is next, where it is in the siddur, and whether to sit or stand. The "Expanded Explanation" includes additional information, such as where the prayer comes from, what the prayer means, or movements we do as we say the prayer. We recommend that you always include the "Simple Transition" to move from one section to the next and that you include "Expanded Explanations" for only a few prayers on any given Shabbat. To determine when to include an "Expanded Explanation," keep in mind the length of the service and the attention span of your participants. As participants become familiar with the material in the "Expanded Explanations," you can present the material as questions to the children rather than simply telling them the information.

For children ages two to six years old, we recommend limiting the service time to about an hour, not including a kiddush. In order to do this, feel free to skip different prayers from week to week. Consider varying the skipped prayers to be sure the children are exposed to as many of the prayers as possible over time.

ROOM SETUP

We recommend setting up your space with an Aron (Ark) or a table with a *tallit* to cover the Torah (real or plush) at the front of the room. To help create an intimate prayer space, we encourage the children to sit on the floor (or carpet square) with their parents for the whole service. For those unable or unwilling to sit on the floor, set out chairs in a wide semicircle facing the Torah. The leader should be in front of the Torah facing the group, sitting on the floor as well. We have found that leaving a large amount of floor space between the Ark and the chairs is the best way to arrange this.

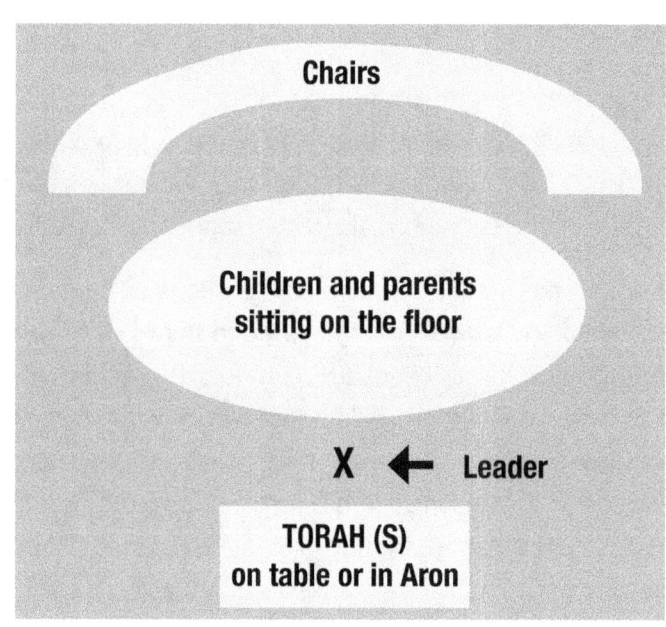

We recommend staying away from auditorium-type seating with chairs in straight lines. This makes participants feel like observers—the opposite of what this service intends to achieve. Additionally, we want the participants to be able to get up and move around at different stages of the service. Chairs in straight lines can make such movement difficult.

If your room is rectangular, we recommend having a wide rather than deep layout. This leaves as little empty space as possible in the back of the room for children to run around or parents to congregate and chat. If you have a very small group, you might consider a large circle.

This service includes an option for story time, during which we encourage you to sit on a chair facing the group to help everyone see and follow the storybook. If sitting on the floor for the whole service does not work for your group, we suggest asking parents and children to sit together on the floor at least for the story so that everyone can see the pictures in the book.

Regardless of the setup that works best for your space, we cannot stress enough the importance of keeping the children with their parents. First, parental modeling is an important component of the learning achieved through this program. Second, when separated (for example, children on floor, parents on chairs), parents quickly lose focus and chat among themselves rather than engaging in the service with their children and ensuring that their children do not infringe on the spiritual experience of other families.

NOISE

Parental noise, rather than children's noise, can become a problem. Let parents know this, and ask for their help in keeping adult noise to a minimum. Consider deputizing parents as "official shushers" (see page 11 of this guide). Use any method with which you are comfortable to convey the importance of retaining parental focus during the service.

STORYBOOKS

The Minyan Katan Shabbat Service includes Torah Time, during which we suggest using songs (included), games (included), and/or books to review general Shabbat information or Torah portion-related material. When you choose to read a book to the participants, read one about Shabbat generally or one that relates to a particular Jewish theme (for example, *mitzvot*, Havdalah, prayers).

Be sure to read through your books ahead of time with your participant demographics in mind and make any necessary changes so the story is appropriate for your group. Don't forget to consider timing and the average age of the children at your service. Skip over text in the books as necessary to shorten them.

KIDDUSH

The Minyan Katan Shabbat Service ends with a small children's kiddush. Consider providing challah, grape juice, and a fruit or cookie snack. Please keep in mind the allergy accommodations generally made in your synagogue community. If possible, keep the food and drink out of the children's sight during the service to avoid distraction. The *b'rachot* (blessings) for the Kiddush and snacks are included at the end of this Leader's Guide and the siddur. If your synagogue has a community kiddush following the main service, invite the families from the children's service to stay and attend. This will help foster a connection between the two services.

Thank you for choosing the Minyan Katan Shabbat Service to help guide your Shabbat morning children's service. Shabbat shalom!

SHABBAT SERVICE

Welcome: Songs and Introduction

SHABBAT SHALOM

To begin the service, sit on the floor, a carpet, or carpet square, and begin singing the welcome song—Shabbat Shalom. Repeat the song three or four times to give everyone a chance to learn it. With each repetition, try a new movement—clap your hands, tap your knees, stomp your feet while sitting. Begin with the song rather than an introduction, as singing tends to capture attention effectively.

SHABBAT SHALOM שַׁבָּת שָׁלוֹם

Have a blessed and peaceful Shabbat.

Shabbat shalom, Shabbat shalom,	שַׁבָּת שָׁלוֹם, שַׁבָּת שָׁלוֹם
Shabbat shalom u'm'vorach x2	שַׁבָּת שָׁלוֹם וּמְבוֹרָךְ 2x
Yai dai dai, yai dai dai dai, yai dai dai dai dai	
Yai dai dai dai, yai dai dai dai	
Shabbat shalom u'm'vorach	שַׁבָּת שָׁלוֹם וּמְבוֹרָךְ

If you have fewer than 10 children, you may want to welcome each child by name. Using the Shabbat Shalom song, after the first "Shabbat Shalom," say "Shabbat Shalom, [insert child's name]" and repeat for each child. Ask parents to say their child's name if the children are too young (or shy) to say their name themselves. After the names have all been said, sing the line "Shabbat shalom u'm'vorach." Conclude with "yai dai dai."

SHABBAT SONGS (CHOOSE ONE)

Pick one of the three songs below to start the service or feel free to substitute other Shabbat songs sung in your community such as "Bim Bam" or "Zum Gali Gali."

1. "It's Shabbat"

Ask children if they have a restful, peaceful Shabbat feeling.

 Does anyone have a restful or peaceful feeling of Shabbat somewhere in their body? Maybe in their feet or in their head?

Take some answers.

"It's Shabbat"—page 4

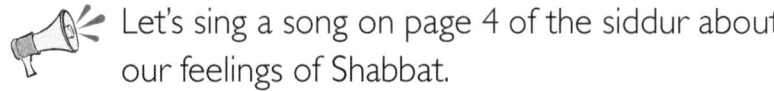 Let's sing a song on page 4 of the siddur about our feelings of Shabbat.

 Be sure to include each body part the children mention during the song even if not listed in the song below.

 If children do not readily participate, tell them you have a feeling of Shabbat in a part of your body and then begin the song. Then try asking the children again during the song.

 Alternative: Depending on the age and knowledge of your group, include the Hebrew words for the body parts. The Hebrew words are noted below directly after the English word for the body part.

IT'S SHABBAT

[tap your head throughout verse]

It's Shabbat—I can feel it in my head/*rosh* x3
Shabbat shalom hay!

[shake your hands out in front of you throughout verse]

It's Shabbat—I can feel it in my hands/*yadayim* x3
Shabbat shalom hay!

in my legs/*raglayim* *[stomp your feet]*; in my belly/*beten* *[pat your belly]*;
in my heart/*leiv* *[tap your heart]*;

[point to the whole group]

It's Shabbat—I can feel it with my friends/*chaveirim* x3
Shabbat shalom hay!

---

2. "It's Time to Make the Challah"

Tell the children about challah. Explain that we will pretend to make it. Page 5.

Before we can welcome Shabbat on Friday night, we have to make sure everything is ready. We need candles, grape juice, and challah—the braided bread we eat on Shabbat. Even if we buy the challah at the store, someone has to make it. Let's pretend to make challah together on page 5.

IT'S TIME TO MAKE THE CHALLAH

It's time to make the challah [point to real or imaginary watch on wrist]

We'll mix and mix and mix [mix imaginary bowl in front of you]

We'll knead and knead [pretend to knead] and let it rise [raise up hands together from floor to head height]

Then braid it in a twist [pretend to braid]

First we'll add the water [pretend to pour water]

We'll mix and mix and mix….

Additional verses: flour, oil, eggs, sugar/honey

Ending: We'll put it in the oven to bake and bake and bake [pretend to put it in the oven]

And then at Shabbat dinner, the Motzi we will make [pretend to take a bite with a loud biting noise]

3. "You'll Never Guess"

 For this next song, use whatever terminology for "synagogue" is most familiar to your participants.

YOU'LL NEVER GUESS

You'll never guess who I met near synagogue/shul/temple today.

Well, I met a duck, he had some friends, and here's what they had to say:

Quack, quack, quack, Shabbat shalom, Shabbat shalom to you. x2

Quack!

You'll never guess who I met near synagogue/shul/temple today.

Well, I met a cow, she had some friends, and here's what they had to say:

Moo, moo, moo, Shabbat shalom, Shabbat shalom to you. x2

Moo!

Additional verses: monkey—oo oo ah ah, lion—roar, sheep—baa

Alternative: If there are fewer than 10 children, go around the room to give each one a chance to suggest an animal for the song. If children suggest an animal that does not make a sound, try to be creative or ask the child for a suggested sound or movement (examples: alligator—open and close arms straight out in front of you saying "chomp" as hands close, bunny/kangaroo—"hop," fish—say "glug")

Introductory Remarks

Greet the participants and introduce yourself. Make sure each family has a siddur.

Welcome everyone. Shabbat Shalom. My name is _____. Before we begin, I want to be sure that each family has a copy of *Siddur Katan*, our prayer book.

 If there are a lot of people or if you have new attendees, add the following.

Ask parents to help keep adult noise to a minimum.

I would like to ask if each parent here could help us keep the adult noise level down to make it easier for the children to hear and participate. I am deputizing each and every one of you as official "shushers"—you are now authorized to "shush" the person next to you if necessary during the service and just blame it on me.

 Add any other welcome details that will help make new people feel comfortable, but keep it short—save announcements for the end.

Ask children what Shabbat is.

Can anyone tell me what Shabbat is?

Take some answers.

Explain that Shabbat, the seventh day of the week, is a day of rest from work because God rested on the seventh day after the work of Creation.

The Torah tells us that when God created the world, God spent six days working very hard to make everything in it, like the sun, moon, animals, oceans, and people. On the seventh day, God looked around and was happy with what God had created during the week. That day, the seventh day, God rested. So we work hard for six days, and on the seventh day—called Shabbat—we rest, just like God did.

Shabbat Service: Introductory Remarks   11

Morning Prayers

MODEH/MODAH ANI

SIMPLE TRANSITION

Modeh/Modah Ani—page 6

Let's start our first prayer—Modeh/Modah Ani—on page 6.

EXPANDED EXPLANATION

Explain that we say Modeh/Modah Ani when we wake up in the morning, to thank God for returning our souls to us on this new day.

We say this prayer when we wake up in the morning. We are thanking God for the part of each one of us that is special, our soul. Boys and men begin the prayer with the word Modeh. Girls and women begin the prayer with the word Modah.

MODEH/MODAH ANI   מוֹדֶה/מוֹדָה אֲנִי

Thank You, God, for bringing my soul back to me.

Modeh/Modah ani l'fanecha	מוֹדֶה/מוֹדָה אֲנִי לְפָנֶיךָ
Melech chai v'kayam	מֶלֶךְ חַי וְקַיָּם
Shehechezarta bi nishmati b'chem'lah	שֶׁהֶחֱזַרְתָּ בִּי נִשְׁמָתִי בְּחֶמְלָה
Rabah emunatecha	רַבָּה אֱמוּנָתֶךָ

MAH TOVU

SIMPLE TRANSITION

Mah Tovu—page 7

Our service continues with Mah Tovu on page 7 of our siddur.

EXPANDED EXPLANATION

Explain that Mah Tovu is about the beautiful tents in which the Jews lived when they traveled through the desert. Participants will stand up and pretend to build tents.

When the Israelites traveled through the desert for 40 years on their way to the land of Israel, they lived in tents. They did not have houses and apartment buildings like we do. The way the Israelites lived their lives in the tents looked beautiful to the people who saw them. That is what the Mah Tovu prayer is about. When we sing Mah Tovu, we are going to pretend to build our own tents with our bodies. Doing this will remind us to live in a way that is beautiful just like our ancestors, the Jewish people who came before us. So, let's stand up and build our tents together starting down low.

There is no need to give directions here; just do the motions and people will follow. Instead of bending over to touch the ground, squat. This avoids the impression that we are bowing down to the ground, which would be inappropriate.

MAH TOVU   מַה טֹּבוּ

Mah Tovu celebrates the beauty of the tents of Israel, used here to represent the beauty of the community of Israel.

Mah tovu	מַה טֹּבוּ
Ohalecha Ya'akov	אֹהָלֶיךָ יַעֲקֹב
Mishk'notecha Yisrael	מִשְׁכְּנֹתֶיךָ יִשְׂרָאֵל

HAL'LU

SIMPLE TRANSITION
Hal'lu—page 8

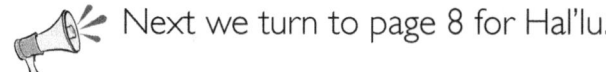 Next we turn to page 8 for Hal'lu.

> **EXPANDED EXPLANATION**
>
> **Explain that Hal'lu is about praising God in different ways. Ask all participants to stand up to dance.**
>
> In Hal'lu, we sing about praising God with singing, dancing, blowing the shofar, and playing musical instruments. So, for this prayer, let's all stand up and dance together.

If there are fewer than 10 people, ask them to hold hands and form a circle. This can help make the individual families feel more connected to one another and part of a unified prayer group. If there are more than 10 people, have participants form small circles with their family members so that it does not become too chaotic. Suggested movements for each verse appear below.

HAL'LU הַלְּלוּ

In Hal'lu, we praise God in different ways. We sing of praising God with musical instruments, such as flutes and cymbals. We marvel that the breath of every creature praises God.

[march to the left]

Hal'luyah, hal'luyah	הַלְלוּיָהּ הַלְלוּיָהּ
Hal'luyah, hal'luyah	הַלְלוּיָהּ הַלְלוּיָהּ
Hal'lu, hal'lu Eil b'kodsho	הַלְלוּ הַלְלוּ אֵל בְּקָדְשׁוֹ
Hal'luhu, hal'luhu birki'a uzo	הַלְלוּהוּ הַלְלוּהוּ בִּרְקִיעַ עֻזּוֹ

[march to the right]

Hal'luhu, hal'luhu	הַלְלוּהוּ הַלְלוּהוּ
Hal'luhu, hal'luhu	הַלְלוּהוּ הַלְלוּהוּ
Hal'luhu, hal'luhu bigvurotav	הַלְלוּהוּ הַלְלוּהוּ בִּגְבוּרֹתָיו
Hal'luhu, hal'luhu k'rov gudlo	הַלְלוּהוּ הַלְלוּהוּ כְּרֹב גֻּדְלוֹ

[let go of hands and jump]

Hal'luhu, hal'luhu	הַלְלוּהוּ הַלְלוּהוּ
Hal'luhu, hal'luhu	הַלְלוּהוּ הַלְלוּהוּ
Hal'luhu, hal'luhu b'teika shofar	הַלְלוּהוּ הַלְלוּהוּ בְּתֵקַע שׁוֹפָר
Hal'luhu, hal'luhu b'neivel v'chinor	הַלְלוּהוּ הַלְלוּהוּ בְּנֵבֶל וְכִנּוֹר

[spin one way and then the other]

Hal'luhu, hal'luhu	הַלְלוּהוּ הַלְלוּהוּ
Hal'luhu, hal'luhu	הַלְלוּהוּ הַלְלוּהוּ
Hal'luhu, hal'luhu b'tof umachol	הַלְלוּהוּ הַלְלוּהוּ בְּתֹף וּמָחוֹל
Hal'luhu, hal'luhu b'minim v'ugav	הַלְלוּהוּ הַלְלוּהוּ בְּמִנִּים וְעֻגָב

[stomp feet in place]

Hal'luhu, hal'luhu	הַלְלוּהוּ הַלְלוּהוּ
Hal'luhu, hal'luhu	הַלְלוּהוּ הַלְלוּהוּ
Hal'luhu, hal'luhu b'tziltz'lei shama	הַלְלוּהוּ הַלְלוּהוּ בְּצִלְצְלֵי שָׁמַע
Hal'luhu, hal'luhu b'tziltz'lei t'ru'ah	הַלְלוּהוּ הַלְלוּהוּ בְּצִלְצְלֵי תְרוּעָה

[hold hands, march to the left, and then to the right]

Kol ha'n'shamah t'haleil Yah, hal'luyah	כֹּל הַנְּשָׁמָה תְּהַלֵּל יָהּ הַלְלוּיָהּ
Kol ha'n'shamah t'haleil Yah, hal'luyah	כֹּל הַנְּשָׁמָה תְּהַלֵּל יָהּ הַלְלוּיָהּ

BAR'CHU

 Some communities use a call and response form of Bar'chu and some do not. Please consult with your clergy to determine the appropriate form of Bar'chu to use in your service.

SIMPLE TRANSITION

Bar'chu—page 9; remain standing, face the Ark.

> Excellent dancing everyone! Now let's all go back to our places, but don't sit down yet. Let's all face the Aron, or Ark, where we keep the Torah and turn to page 9 for Bar'chu.

EXPANDED EXPLANATION #1

Explain that Bar'chu is a call to prayer as a group. Explain the choreography as well.

> The Bar'chu is the way a leader of a prayer service like ours calls out to the people to say, "OK, everyone, it's time for us to pray as a group now."
>
> This prayer includes some movements. Let's go through them before we actually say the prayer. We start with our feet together. Then we bow forward on the first word, bar'chu, and stand up straight and tall for God's name, Adonai.

EXPANDED EXPLANATION #2—Include only if you are using the call and response form of Bar'chu

Explain the call and response used in Bar'chu.

> Bar'chu is done as a call and response. The prayer leader calls out to the people that it is time to pray together, and the people answer the leader. So I start by singing the first line. You respond together with the next line. Then I repeat that line myself. We finish this part with a longer *b'rachah*, or blessing, together. So, let's give it a try.

 If you are not using the call and response form of Bar'chu, sing the first Leader's line and the Congregation's line together as a group. Skip the second Leader's line and conclude with the Leader & Congregation line.

16 Siddur Katan Leader's Guide

BAR'CHU בָּרְכוּ

In Bar'chu, we praise God as the source of all blessings for all time. We praise God, Creator of light and darkness, Maker of peace, and Creator of all things.

Leader:

Bar'chu et Adonai ha'm'vorach

בָּרְכוּ אֶת יְיָ הַמְבֹרָךְ

Congregation:

Baruch Adonai ha'm'vorach l'olam va'ed

בָּרוּךְ יְיָ הַמְבֹרָךְ לְעוֹלָם וָעֶד

Leader:

Baruch Adonai ha'm'vorach l'olam va'ed

בָּרוּךְ יְיָ הַמְבֹרָךְ לְעוֹלָם וָעֶד

Leader & Congregation:

Baruch Atah Adonai Eloheinu Melech ha'olam

בָּרוּךְ אַתָּה יְיָ אֱלֹהֵינוּ מֶלֶךְ הָעוֹלָם

Yotzeir or uvorei choshech

יוֹצֵר אוֹר וּבוֹרֵא חֹשֶׁךְ

Oseh shalom uvorei et hakol

עֹשֶׂה שָׁלוֹם וּבוֹרֵא אֶת הַכֹּל

Some communities sit at this point in the service and others remain standing through the Sh'ma. Please consult with your clergy to determine the custom of your community. Please advise families to sit or stand accordingly.

Shabbat Service: Morning Prayers

OR CHADASH

SIMPLE TRANSITION

Or Chadash—page 10

> Next, we turn to page 10 for Or Chadash.

EXPANDED EXPLANATION

Explain that this prayer is about God as the Creator of light.

> Or means "light." Chadash means "new." In Or Chadash, we ask God, who is the Creator of all things, including light, for a new light to shine on Israel. When we talk about light in this prayer we don't mean the light we get from light bulbs. We mean the light of peace and happiness.

OR CHADASH   אוֹר חָדָשׁ

Let a new light shine on Zion and may we all be able to see its beauty. Praised are You, God, who makes the light.

Or chadash al Tziyon ta'ir x2	אוֹר חָדָשׁ עַל צִיּוֹן תָּאִיר 2x
V'nizkeh chulanu m'heirah l'oro x2	וְנִזְכֶּה כֻלָּנוּ מְהֵרָה לְאוֹרוֹ 2x
Baruch Atah Adonai	בָּרוּךְ אַתָּה יְיָ
Yotzeir ham'orot	יוֹצֵר הַמְּאוֹרוֹת

SH'MA

 Some communities do not cover their eyes for the Sh'ma. Additionally, some communities say the Baruch sheim k'vod line out loud together. Please consult with your clergy to determine which practice is appropriate for your service.

SIMPLE TRANSITION

Sh'ma—page 11

 Now let's turn to page 11 of our siddur. For this prayer we cover our eyes.

EXPANDED EXPLANATION #1

Tell the participants that the Sh'ma states that God is one. The V'ahavta is from the Torah and tells us to love God with all of our heart and soul. It tells us to say the Sh'ma when we wake and before we go to sleep, and to teach these words to our children. Explain that it also tells us to put the words on our doorpost, which we do in a mezuzah.

"Listen up, everyone! Listen up!" That's what the Sh'ma is saying. "All the people of Israel, listen! God is our God and God is one." The longer paragraph that comes next, the V'ahavta, is actually straight from the Torah telling us to love God with all of our heart, all of our soul, and all of our strength. It tells us to say the Sh'ma when we wake up each day and before we go to sleep each night. It also tells us to teach the Sh'ma to our children.

Did you know that the V'ahavta also tell us to put the Sh'ma on our doorposts? Who knows the name of the thing we hang on our doorpost? *[A mezuzah.]* The Sh'ma is written on a piece of special paper called parchment inside each mezuzah. *[Point or go over to the mezuzah on the door if there is one in view.]*

EXPANDED EXPLANATION #2—If your community covers their eyes for the Sh'ma

Explain that we cover our eyes so we can concentrate on God and the prayer, and really listen to what we are saying. Instruct participants to say the first line out loud together, the second line quietly, and the last part out loud together.

 Who knows what we do with our hands when we say the Sh'ma?
Does anyone know why?
To say the Sh'ma, we cover our eyes so that we can really concentrate on God and the prayer we are saying and have no distractions. We say the words of the Sh'ma line loudly and clearly together. For the next line, we uncover our eyes and say the words quietly in a whisper. Then we say the longer part, the V'ahavta, out loud together. Let's try it.

Sing the first two lines of this prayer especially SLOWLY to give everyone a chance to follow along.

SH'MA שְׁמַע

The people of Israel are told to hear as the Sh'ma proclaims God's oneness and God's greatness forever.

Sh'ma Yisrael Adonai Eloheinu
    Adonai echad
שְׁמַע יִשְׂרָאֵל יְיָ אֱלֹהֵינוּ יְיָ אֶחָד

Baruch sheim k'vod, malchuto
    l'olam va'ed
בָּרוּךְ שֵׁם כְּבוֹד מַלְכוּתוֹ לְעוֹלָם וָעֶד

In the V'ahavta, we are instructed to love God with all of our heart, might, and soul. We are told to teach these words to our children, to think of them wherever we are, before we go to sleep and when we wake up. We are to wear reminders of these words on our hands and head (in tefillin). We are to write them on our doorposts and gates (in mezuzot).

V'ahavta et Adonai Elohecha
וְאָהַבְתָּ אֵת יְיָ אֱלֹהֶיךָ

b'chol l'vav'cha uv'chol nafsh'cha
    uv'chol m'odecha
בְּכָל לְבָבְךָ וּבְכָל נַפְשְׁךָ וּבְכָל מְאֹדֶךָ

V'hayu had'varim ha'eileh
וְהָיוּ הַדְּבָרִים הָאֵלֶּה

asher anochi m'tzavcha hayom
    al l'vavecha
אֲשֶׁר אָנֹכִי מְצַוְּךָ הַיּוֹם עַל לְבָבֶךָ

V'shinantam l'vanecha, v'dibarta bam
וְשִׁנַּנְתָּם לְבָנֶיךָ וְדִבַּרְתָּ בָּם

B'shivt'cha b'veitecha, uv'lecht'cha
    vaderech
בְּשִׁבְתְּךָ בְּבֵיתֶךָ וּבְלֶכְתְּךָ בַדֶּרֶךְ

Uv'shochb'cha uv'kumecha
וּבְשָׁכְבְּךָ וּבְקוּמֶךָ

Uk'shartam l'ot al yadecha
וּקְשַׁרְתָּם לְאוֹת עַל יָדֶךָ

V'hayu l'totafot bein einecha
וְהָיוּ לְטֹטָפֹת בֵּין עֵינֶיךָ

Uch'tavtam al m'zuzot beitecha
    uvish'arecha
וּכְתַבְתָּם עַל מְזֻזוֹת בֵּיתֶךָ וּבִשְׁעָרֶיךָ

MI CHAMOCHAH

SIMPLE TRANSITION

Mi Chamochah—page 12

 Next let's turn to page 12 for Mi Chamochah.

EXPANDED EXPLANATION

Explain that Mi Chamochah asks who is like God. No one! The words are from the Torah and part of the song the Israelites sang praising God after they were freed from Egypt.

Who is like God? Me? You? No. No one in the whole world is like God. That's what we say in this prayer. The words of this prayer come from the Torah, which describes how, when God freed the Israelites from slavery in Egypt, the people sang a song to God to say thank you. In this part of the song, the Israelites say that there is no one like God, who does amazing miracles.

MI CHAMOCHAH   מִי כָמֹכָה

Who can compare in power or holiness to God, who does awesome deeds?

Mi chamochah ba'eilim Adonai	מִי כָמֹכָה בָּאֵלִם יְיָ
Mi kamochah nedar bakodesh	מִי כָּמֹכָה נֶאְדָּר בַּקֹּדֶשׁ
Nora t'hilot oseh fele	נוֹרָא תְהִלֹּת עֹשֵׂה פֶלֶא

Shabbat Service: Morning Prayers

AMIDAH

 If you choose to include Expanded Explanation #1 or #2, we suggest doing so before the Simple Transition.

EXPANDED EXPLANATION #1

Introduce the concept of prayer to participants, asking what it means and what it is for.

📢 Who knows what a prayer is? Who are we talking to? Why? What are we saying? In a prayer, we are talking to God. We ask for things, say thank you for things, and say sorry for things.

Ask children what they want to say to God in a prayer.

📢 What do you want to talk to God about? *[Take some answers. If no one has any ideas, start them off with suggestions, such as asking for a nice day with their families, asking for help with something that is hard, and saying thank you for their families or friends.]*

Introduce the Amidah, explaining that it's a chance to stand and pray quietly to God ourselves or with our families.

📢 We have been saying a lot of prayers to God together this morning. Sometimes, though, we like to talk to God ourselves, quietly, on our own or with our families. We can do that now in the next prayer, called the Amidah.

EXPANDED EXPLANATION #2

Explain the steps and the bowing motions in the Amidah.

📢 The name of this next prayer—Amidah—comes from the Hebrew word for standing because we stand for this prayer.

Before we start the Amidah, we take three steps backward then three steps forward. That is the way people used to come to speak to a king or a queen. So, we are treating God like a king or queen as we say our prayer.

Next, we put our feet together. We bend our knees on the first word, Baruch. We bow at the waist on the second word, Atah. We stand up straight and tall for the next word, the name of God, Adonai.

22 Siddur Katan Leader's Guide

SIMPLE TRANSITION

Amidah—page 13. Explain that we will take a few moments after singing together to talk to God personally, alone or with our families.

🔊 Let's all stand up together for the Amidah on page 13. We will begin by saying the prayer out loud together and then spend a few moments quietly talking to God ourselves and with our families about whatever is on our minds.

👆 *Please consult with your clergy to determine whether it is appropriate in your community to include the bracketed words about the Imahot, "foremothers," whether to say u'foked in the next-to-last line, and whether to say u'foked or v'ezrat in the last line.*

AMIDAH עֲמִידָה

We praise God—our God, and God of our forefathers Abraham, Isaac, and Jacob [and our foremothers Sarah, Rebecca, Rachel, and Leah]. God is great and strong. God remembers all that our ancestors have done and will bring a redeemer to their children. Praised are You, God, the shield of Abraham and guardian/helper of Sarah.

Baruch Atah Adonai Eloheinu veilohei avoteinu [v'imoteinu]	בָּרוּךְ אַתָּה יְיָ אֱלֹהֵינוּ וֵאלֹהֵי אֲבוֹתֵינוּ [וְאִמּוֹתֵינוּ]
Elohei Avraham, Elohei Yitzchak, veilohei Ya'akov	אֱלֹהֵי אַבְרָהָם אֱלֹהֵי יִצְחָק וֵאלֹהֵי יַעֲקֹב
[Elohei Sarah, Elohei Rivkah, Elohei Rachel, veilohei Le'ah]	[אֱלֹהֵי שָׂרָה אֱלֹהֵי רִבְקָה אֱלֹהֵי רָחֵל וֵאלֹהֵי לֵאָה]
Ha'eil hagadol hagibor v'hanora Eil elyon	הָאֵל הַגָּדוֹל הַגִּבּוֹר וְהַנּוֹרָא אֵל עֶלְיוֹן
Gomeil chasadim tovim v'koneih hakol	גּוֹמֵל חֲסָדִים טוֹבִים וְקוֹנֵה הַכֹּל
V'zocheir chasdei avot [v'imahot]	וְזוֹכֵר חַסְדֵי אָבוֹת [וְאִמָּהוֹת]
Umeivi go'eil [geulah] livnei v'neihem	וּמֵבִיא גוֹאֵל [גְּאֻלָּה] לִבְנֵי בְנֵיהֶם
L'ma'an sh'mo b'ahavah	לְמַעַן שְׁמוֹ בְּאַהֲבָה
Melech ozeir [u'fokeid] umoshi'a umagein	מֶלֶךְ עוֹזֵר [וּפוֹקֵד] וּמוֹשִׁיעַ וּמָגֵן
Baruch Atah Adonai magein Avraham [u'foked/v'ezrat Sarah]	בָּרוּךְ אַתָּה יְיָ מָגֵן אַבְרָהָם [וּפוֹקֵד/וְעֶזְרַת שָׂרָה]

Shabbat Service: Morning Prayers

After 15 to 30 seconds of quiet time, transition to Oseh Shalom.

OSEH SHALOM

 Please consult with your clergy to determine whether it is appropriate in your community to include the bracketed words in Oseh Shalom.

SIMPLE TRANSITION

Oseh Shalom—page 14; all sit.

 Let's all take our seats and end the Amidah with Oseh Shalom on page 14.

EXPANDED EXPLANATION

Explain that Oseh Shalom asks God to bring peace to us and to all people.

We sing the next prayer together to ask God, the one who brings peace, to bring peace to all of us here, to all of Israel, and to people everywhere.

OSEH SHALOM עֹשֶׂה שָׁלוֹם

May God, who brings peace to the universe, bring peace to us and to all of Israel.

Oseh shalom bimromav	עֹשֶׂה שָׁלוֹם בִּמְרוֹמָיו
Hu ya'aseh shalom aleinu	הוּא יַעֲשֶׂה שָׁלוֹם עָלֵינוּ
V'al kol Yisrael	וְעַל כָּל יִשְׂרָאֵל
[v'al kol yoshvei teiveil]	[וְעַל כָּל יוֹשְׁבֵי תֵבֵל]
V'imru amen	וְאִמְרוּ אָמֵן

Torah Service: Prayers, Activities, and Songs

 If you include Expanded Explanation #1 or #2, do so before the Simple Transition.

EXPANDED EXPLANATION #1

Explain that every Shabbat we read a part of the Torah in the main service. The Torah teaches us how the Jews used to live and how to live now.

🔊 Next is our Torah service. Every Shabbat, in the big, main service, we read from the Torah. Each week we read a little bit more. It takes a whole year to read the whole Torah. The Torah tells us a lot about God. It has stories about what happened to the Jewish people a long time ago. It also has a lot of rules in it that teach us how to be good, kind people. We are going to start our Torah service the same way we do in the big service and then do some different activities to help us learn about the Torah.

EXPANDED EXPLANATION #2

Tell the children about the Aron.

🔊 Has anyone ever had anything so important to them that they kept it in a special place? The Torah is like a treasure to the Jewish people, so we keep it in a very special place. That place is called an Aron, or Ark. To show how important it is, we stand facing the Aron when we pray. Since the Torah is so important to us, and because it is all about God, we stand up when the Aron is open and when we take the Torah out of its special place.

SIMPLE TRANSITION

Torah Service—page 15; stand up, face Aron.

 Let's all stand up, face the Aron, or Ark, and turn to page 15.

VAY'HI BINSO'A HA'ARON

 Some communities begin with Ki miTziyon on the fourth line below. Please consult with your clergy to determine the appropriate starting place for your community.

VAY'HI BINSO'A HA'ARON   וַיְהִי בִּנְסֹעַ הָאָרֹן

When the Ark traveled with the Israelites through the desert, Moses would say that, with God's strength, God's enemies would be scattered. The Torah will go forth from Zion and God's word from Jerusalem. We praise God for giving us the Torah.

Vay'hi binso'a ha'aron vayomer Moshe	וַיְהִי בִּנְסֹעַ הָאָרֹן וַיֹּאמֶר מֹשֶׁה
Kumah Adonai v'yafutzu oy'vecha	קוּמָה יְיָ וְיָפֻצוּ אֹיְבֶיךָ
V'yanusu m'sanecha mipanecha	וְיָנֻסוּ מְשַׂנְאֶיךָ מִפָּנֶיךָ
Ki miTziyon teitzei Torah x2	כִּי מִצִּיּוֹן תֵּצֵא תוֹרָה 2x
Ud'var Adonai mirushalayim	וּדְבַר יְיָ מִירוּשָׁלָיִם
Baruch shenatan Torah Torah x2	בָּרוּךְ שֶׁנָּתַן תּוֹרָה תּוֹרָה 2x
L'amo Yisrael bik'dushato	לְעַמּוֹ יִשְׂרָאֵל בִּקְדֻשָּׁתוֹ

"TORAH TZIVAH LANU MOSHE"

This is a great opportunity for kids to be part of a Torah parade. Carry a real Torah or a large plush stuffed Torah and lead the families on a parade around the room singing "Torah Tzivah Lanu Moshe." Continue to repeat the song for the duration of the parade.

SIMPLE TRANSITION

Ask the participants to follow the Torah for a parade and sing "Torah Tzivah Lanu Moshe" on page 15.

Follow the Torah for our Torah parade, everyone. We are going to sing "Torah Tzivah Lanu Moshe" on page 15 of our siddur.

If there is not enough room for all participants to march safely in a parade, have one person walk around the room with the Torah so that everyone gets to see it. Participants can clap their hands and offer the Torah a real kiss or an air kiss when it is carried past them.

TORAH TZIVAH LANU MOSHE — תּוֹרָה צִוָּה לָנוּ מֹשֶׁה

We rejoice that Moses received the Torah, which God commands us to follow.

Torah Torah Torah	תּוֹרָה תּוֹרָה תּוֹרָה
Torah Torah Torah	תּוֹרָה תּוֹרָה תּוֹרָה
Torah tzivah lanu Moshe	תּוֹרָה צִוָּה לָנוּ מֹשֶׁה

[repeat above 3 lines]

Torah Torah Torah Torah	תּוֹרָה תּוֹרָה תּוֹרָה תּוֹרָה
Torah tzivah lanu Moshe	תּוֹרָה צִוָּה לָנוּ מֹשֶׁה

[repeat above 2 lines]

Alternative: To give families an opportunity to join the main service, you may want to coordinate with the rabbi or cantor ahead of time to have the children and parents follow behind the Torah as it is carried around the sanctuary or other prayer space before or after the Torah reading. This often requires having an adult let you know the appropriate time to enter the main service—regardless of where you are in the children's service—so the children are not bored and potentially disruptive in the main service. Additionally, be sure to announce to the parents beforehand that the children's service will continue in the room where it began after the Torah parade in the main service is over.

Instruct participants to be seated for Torah Time.

Excellent, everybody. Now let's have a seat for Torah Time.

Shabbat Service: Torah Service

Torah Time

 Depending on how much time you have, include one or more of the activities below.

READ A SHABBAT STORY

For a list of suggested Shabbat and Jewish-themed books, visit www.behrmanhouse.com/minyankatan/Shabbat.

 After the story is over, ask the children a few questions so they can think about a moral or something they learned from the story.

PLAY A SHABBAT OR JEWISH-THEMED GAME

Torah Traveler—See the Torah Traveler game template for instructions and materials at www.behrmanhouse.com/minyankatan/Shabbat.

Kippah, Candle, Cup—See the Kippah, Candle, Cup game template for instructions and materials at www.behrmanhouse.com/minyankatan/Shabbat.

Shabbat Shadow Shapes—See the Shabbat Shadow Shapes game template for instructions and materials at www.behrmanhouse.com/minyankatan/Shabbat.

SING SHABBAT SONGS

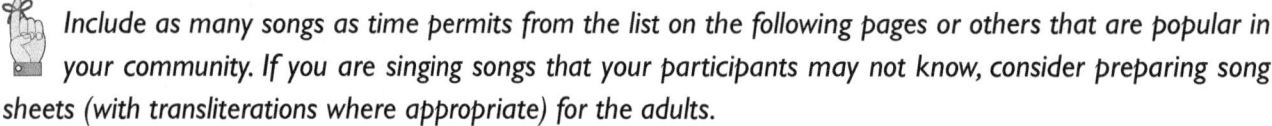 *Include as many songs as time permits from the list on the following pages or others that are popular in your community. If you are singing songs that your participants may not know, consider preparing song sheets (with transliterations where appropriate) for the adults.*

 If the children have been sitting for most of Torah Time, be sure to sing a song or two with movement.

1. "Do You Know"

Explain a mitzvah.

A mitzvah is doing something that we are told to do in the Torah. It is often something good or nice for someone else. We all know how to do a mitzvah, so let's sing it in our song. Then you can tell me some different mitzvot that we can put into our song! Repeat after me. I say, "Do you know," then you say, "Do you know."

DO YOU KNOW

Do you know *[participants: Do you know]* x2
Do you know how to do a mitzvah
Do you know *[participants: Do you know]* x2
I know how to do a mitzvah

A mitzvah's doing something good
Something the Torah says we should
Like giving tzedakah
I know how to do a mitzvah

Do you know *[participants: Do you know]* x2
Do you know how to do a mitzvah
Do you know *[participants: Do you know]* x2
Do you know how to do a mitzvah

A mitzvah's doing something good
Something the Torah says we should
Like *[add in mitzvot the participants suggest]*
I know how to do a mitzvah

Do you know *[participants: Do you know]* x2
Do you know how to do a mitzvah
Do you know *[participants: Do you know]* x2
I know how to do a mitzvah

Shabbat Service: Torah Service

2. "Torah"

Ask everyone to say "Torah" after you say "Torah" and to tap their knees.

> I need everyone to be my echo for this next song. I want you all to say "Torah" after I say "Torah." And don't forget to be loud! Let's try it.

TORAH

[Say "Torah" once or twice and have families echo.]

Now let's all tap our knees to start a good beat for our song.

Where do we learn stories of Jews of long ago

How they used to live their lives and all they used to know

It's in the Torah *[participants: Torah!]*, in the Torah *[participants: Torah!]*, in the Torah *[participants: Torah!]*

In six days God made the world, boy, God worked a lot

The seventh day God rested and that's where we get Shabbat

It's in the Torah *[participants: Torah!]*, in the Torah *[participants: Torah!]*, in the Torah *[participants: Torah!]*

The Jews were slaves in Egypt, God said let them go away

God gave us 10 good rules and we still follow them today

It's in the Torah *[participants: Torah!]*, it's the Torah *[participants: Torah!]*, it's the Torah *[participants: Torah!]*

The five books of Moses, B'reisheet, Sh'mot, and then

Vayikra and B'midbar, D'varim then start again

It's in the Torah *[participants: Torah!]*, it's the Torah *[participants: Torah!]*, it's the Torah *[participants: Torah!]*

It's in the Torah *[participants: Torah!]*, it's the Torah *[participants: Torah!]*, it's the Torah *[participants: Torah!]*

3. "Shabbat at Home"

Explain about welcoming Shabbat at home.

📢 When we welcome Shabbat at home on Friday nights, we light the Shabbat candles, drink some grape juice, and eat challah. Each of these has a special blessing we say. Let's sing a song about this.

SHABBAT AT HOME

[pretend to light candles with hands] **Light the candles,** *[cover eyes]* **say the blessing**

[hold up wine cup] **Say the Kiddush,** *[pretend to sip from cup]* **drink the wine**

[hands out together as if over challah] **Say the Motzi,** *[pretend to eat]* **eat the challah**

[rub belly] **Now it's dinner time**

[tap legs or clap hands] **Because it's Shabbat at home, Shabbat at home**

Shabbat shalom

Shabbat at home, Shabbat at home

Shabbat shalom

---

4. "Every Friday Night"

Explain Shabbat is like a gift. Ask families to put their hands on their neighbors' backs and sway.

📢 Shabbat is a wonderful time to be with our families and spend quiet time together. It's like a present from God that we get every week. Let's all put our hands lightly on each other's backs and sway side to side for our next song.

EVERY FRIDAY NIGHT

Every Friday night, as the sun begins to set

God gives me a present—Shabbat the day of rest

So as I watch the Shabbat candles shine

Have a day of family time

I know Shabbat's a gift from God that's mine

I know Shabbat's a gift from God that's mine

EITZ CHAYIM HI

SIMPLE TRANSITION

Eitz Chayim Hi—page 16; stand, face the Ark.

📢 Let's stand and turn to face the Aron for the end of the Torah service with Eitz Chayim Hi on page 16.

EXPANDED EXPLANATION

Introduce the idea of the Torah as a tree of life.

📢 In this prayer, we say the Torah is like a tree of life for us when we follow it. As we grow, it stays with us.

EITZ CHAYIM HI — עֵץ חַיִּים הִיא

In this prayer, we compare the Torah to a tree of life for those who embrace it. We ask for help returning to God.

Eitz chayim hi	עֵץ חַיִּים הִיא
Lamachazikim bah	לַמַּחֲזִיקִים בָּהּ
V'tom'cheha m'ushar	וְתֹמְכֶיהָ מְאֻשָּׁר
D'racheha darchei no'am	דְּרָכֶיהָ דַּרְכֵי נֹעַם
V'chol n'tivoteha shalom	וְכָל נְתִיבוֹתֶיהָ שָׁלוֹם
Hashiveinu Adonai eilecha v'nashuvah	הֲשִׁיבֵנוּ יְיָ אֵלֶיךָ וְנָשׁוּבָה
Chadeish yameinu k'kedem	חַדֵּשׁ יָמֵינוּ כְּקֶדֶם

Concluding Prayers and Songs

 The order of the concluding prayers varies among congregations. Please consult with your clergy to determine the appropriate order of the concluding prayers in your community.

EIN KEILOHEINU

SIMPLE TRANSITION

Ein Keiloheinu—page 17; all sit.  Let's all have a seat as our service continues with Ein Keiloheinu on page 17 of our siddur.

EIN KEILOHEINU · אֵין כֵּאלֹהֵינוּ

We thank and praise God and say that there is none like our God.

Ein Keiloheinu, ein Kadoneinu	אֵין כֵּאלֹהֵינוּ, אֵין כַּאדוֹנֵינוּ
Ein K'malkeinu, ein K'moshi'einu	אֵין כְּמַלְכֵּנוּ, אֵין כְּמוֹשִׁיעֵנוּ
Mi Cheiloheinu, mi Chadoneinu	מִי כֵאלֹהֵינוּ, מִי כַאדוֹנֵינוּ
Mi Ch'malkeinu, mi Ch'moshi'einu	מִי כְמַלְכֵּנוּ, מִי כְמוֹשִׁיעֵנוּ
Nodeh Leiloheinu, nodeh Ladoneinu	נוֹדֶה לֵאלֹהֵינוּ, נוֹדֶה לַאדוֹנֵינוּ
Nodeh L'malkeinu, nodeh L'moshi'einu	נוֹדֶה לְמַלְכֵּנוּ, נוֹדֶה לְמוֹשִׁיעֵנוּ
Baruch Eloheinu, baruch Adoneinu	בָּרוּךְ אֱלֹהֵינוּ, בָּרוּךְ אֲדוֹנֵינוּ
Baruch Malkeinu, baruch Moshi'einu	בָּרוּךְ מַלְכֵּנוּ, בָּרוּךְ מוֹשִׁיעֵנוּ
Atah hu Eloheinu, Atah hu Adoneinu	אַתָּה הוּא אֱלֹהֵינוּ, אַתָּה הוּא אֲדוֹנֵינוּ
Atah hu Malkeinu, Atah hu Moshi'einu	אַתָּה הוּא מַלְכֵּנוּ, אַתָּה הוּא מוֹשִׁיעֵנוּ
Atah hu she'hiktiru avoteinu	אַתָּה הוּא שֶׁהִקְטִירוּ אֲבוֹתֵינוּ
L'fanecha et k'toret hasamim	לְפָנֶיךָ אֶת קְטֹרֶת הַסַּמִּים

ALEINU

SIMPLE TRANSITION

Aleinu—page 18; all stand.  We stand for Aleinu on page 18 and face the Ark.

ALEINU עָלֵינוּ

In Aleinu, we praise God for making us different than others in the world.
We bend our knees and bow to thank God, the Holy One.

Aleinu l'shabei'ach la'adon hakol	עָלֵינוּ לְשַׁבֵּחַ לַאֲדוֹן הַכֹּל
Lateit g'dulah l'yotzeir b'reisheet	לָתֵת גְּדֻלָּה לְיוֹצֵר בְּרֵאשִׁית
Shelo asanu k'goyei ha'aratzot	שֶׁלֹּא עָשָׂנוּ כְּגוֹיֵי הָאֲרָצוֹת
V'lo samanu k'mishp'chot ha'adamah	וְלֹא שָׂמָנוּ כְּמִשְׁפְּחוֹת הָאֲדָמָה
Shelo sam chelkeinu kahem	שֶׁלֹּא שָׂם חֶלְקֵנוּ כָּהֶם
V'goraleinu k'chol hamonam	וְגוֹרָלֵנוּ כְּכָל הֲמוֹנָם

Va'anachnu kor'im u'mishtachavim — וַאֲנַחְנוּ כּוֹרְעִים וּמִשְׁתַּחֲוִים

u'modim — וּמוֹדִים

Lifnei Melech malchei ham'lachim — לִפְנֵי מֶלֶךְ מַלְכֵי הַמְּלָכִים
Hakadosh baruch hu — הַקָּדוֹשׁ בָּרוּךְ הוּא

FINAL PRAYER/SONG (CHOOSE ONE)

SIMPLE TRANSITION

All sit. Make any relevant announcements including about a kiddush, if you are having one, and the date of the next children's service.

 Let's all have a seat before we finish our service.

[Make any relevant announcements including asking participants to join you for a kiddush after the final song/prayer and the date of the next children's service.]

 Pick one of the three choices below to end the service.

1. Adon Olam

SIMPLE TRANSITION

Adon Olam—page 19.

 Let's turn to page 19 for Adon Olam.

EXPANDED EXPLANATION

Introduce instruments for Adon Olam.

It's been such fun sharing Shabbat together. Let's all take out our magical musical instrument bags for our Adon Olam orchestra. *[Pretend to open up a big bag in front of you.]*

First we have the trombone. Let's give it a try. *[Pretend to take a trombone out of your bag. Demonstrate by holding your fists next to each other in front of your mouth sliding one fist away from your face and back again].*

Next is the flute. *[Pretend to take the flute out of your bag. Demonstrate by pretending to move your fingers on a flute to the side of your face.]*

We also need our drums. *[Pretend to take a heavy drum set out of your bag. Demonstrate by tapping your knees alternating left and right.]*

Last we have our guitar. *[Pretend to take a guitar from your bag. Demonstrate by pretending to strum a guitar in front of your stomach.]*

ADON OLAM אֲדוֹן עוֹלָם

*Adon Olam recognizes the timelessness of God and God's relationship with us.
We put our spirits in God's hands and then have nothing to fear.*

Adon olam *[trombone]*	אֲדוֹן עוֹלָם
asher malach *[trombone]*	אֲשֶׁר מָלַךְ
b'terem kol *[flute]*	בְּטֶרֶם כָּל
y'tzir nivra *[drums]*	יְצִיר נִבְרָא
L'eit na'asah *[trombone]*	לְעֵת נַעֲשָׂה
v'cheftzo kol *[trombone]*	בְחֶפְצוֹ כֹּל
azai Melech *[guitar]*	אֲזַי מֶלֶךְ
sh'mo nikra *[guitar]*	שְׁמוֹ נִקְרָא
V'acharei kichlot hakol l'vado	וְאַחֲרֵי כִּכְלוֹת הַכֹּל לְבַדּוֹ
yimloch nora	יִמְלוֹךְ נוֹרָא
V'hu hayah v'hu hoveh v'hu	וְהוּא הָיָה וְהוּא הֹוֶה וְהוּא
yih'yeh b'tifarah	יִהְיֶה בְּתִפְאָרָה
V'hu echad v'ein sheini l'hamshil	וְהוּא אֶחָד וְאֵין שֵׁנִי לְהַמְשִׁיל
lo l'hachbirah	לוֹ לְהַחְבִּירָה
B'li reisheet b'li tachlit v'lo	בְּלִי רֵאשִׁית בְּלִי תַכְלִית וְלוֹ
ha'oz v'hamisrah	הָעֹז וְהַמִּשְׂרָה
V'hu Eili v'chai go'ali v'tzur chevli	וְהוּא אֵלִי וְחַי גֹּאֲלִי וְצוּר חֶבְלִי
b'eit tzarah	בְּעֵת צָרָה
V'hu nisi umanos li m'nat kosi	וְהוּא נִסִּי וּמָנוֹס לִי מְנָת כּוֹסִי
b'yom ekra	בְּיוֹם אֶקְרָא
B'yado afkid ruchi b'eit	בְּיָדוֹ אַפְקִיד רוּחִי בְּעֵת
ishan v'a'irah	אִישָׁן וְאָעִירָה
V'im ruchi g'viy'ati Adonai	וְעִם רוּחִי גְּוִיָּתִי יְיָ
li v'lo ira	לִי וְלֹא אִירָא

2. "3 Stars In the Sky"

SIMPLE TRANSITION

"3 Stars In the Sky"—page 20.  Please turn to page 20 for "3 Stars In the Sky."

EXPANDED EXPLANATION

Explain that Shabbat is over when there are three stars in the sky on Saturday night and that the prayer we say when Shabbat is over is called Havdalah.

 It's been such fun sharing Shabbat together. Who can tell me when Shabbat starts?
[Take some answers.]
Does anyone know when Shabbat ends?
[Take some answers.]
Shabbat ends on Saturday night when there are three stars in the sky. Once there are three stars in the sky, Shabbat is over and we say a special prayer called Havdalah. Let's pretend it's nighttime and count our stars.

3 STARS IN THE SKY

[hold up 1 finger] 1 star in the sky, 1 star in the sky, *[open and close fingers on 1 hand like a blinking star]* 1 star in the nighttime darkness, 1 star in the sky

Is it time for Havdalah? *[pause to let children answer]* No!— not 'til 3 stars shine above

[look as if your eyes are closed and sit with your hands in your lap] So close your eyes and feel Shabbat, *[pause]* with us for its last few minutes.

[hold up 2 fingers] 2 stars in the sky, 2 stars in the sky, *[open and close fingers on both hands like blinking stars]* 2 stars in the nighttime darkness, 2 stars in the sky

Is it time for Havdalah? *[pause to let children answer]* No!— not 'til 3 stars shine above

[look as if your eyes are closed and sit with your hands in your lap] So close your eyes and feel Shabbat, *[pause]* with us for its last few minutes.

[hold up 3 fingers] 3 stars in the sky, 3 stars in the sky, *[open and close fingers on both hands like blinking stars]* 3 stars in the nighttime darkness, 3 stars in the sky

Is it time for Havdalah? *[pause to let children answer]* Yes!— now that 3 stars shine above

[look as if your eyes are closed and sit with your hands in your lap] So close your eyes and feel Shabbat, *[pause]* with us for its last few minutes.

[hold up 1 finger] 1 star in the sky, *[hold up 2 fingers]* 2 stars in the sky, *[hold up 3 fingers]* 3 stars in the sky—hamavdil bein kodesh l'chol.

3. "Hamavdil"

SIMPLE TRANSITION

"Hamavdil"—page 21.

 Please turn to page 21 for "Hamavdil."

EXPANDED EXPLANATION

Explain that Shabbat is over on Saturday night and that the prayer we say when Shabbat is over is called Havdalah. Introduce the last four words—hamavdil bein kodesh l'chol.

It's been such fun sharing Shabbat together. When Shabbat ends on Saturday night we say a prayer called Havdalah. During this prayer, we say a blessing over a big, special candle, grape juice, and sweet smelling spices held in a beautiful box or container.

Havdalah is about the difference between things that are holy, or about God, and things that are ordinary, or not about God. The song we are going to end with is the last four words of the Havdalah prayer. Try saying the words after me—hamavdil bein kodesh l'chol. That's the whole song!

HAMAVDIL הַמַבְדִיל

In this song, we praise God for differentiating between things that are holy and things that are secular.

Hama-hama-hamavdil x3	הַמַ-הַמַ-הַמַבְדִיל 3x
Hamavdil bein kodesh l'chol	הַמַבְדִיל בֵּין קֹדֶשׁ לְחוֹל
Hamavdil bein kodesh, bein kodesh l'chol x2	הַמַבְדִיל בֵּין קֹדֶשׁ בֵּין קֹדֶשׁ לְחוֹל 2x

Kiddush Blessings

BEFORE DRINKING GRAPE JUICE:

Baruch Atah Adonai	בָּרוּךְ אַתָּה יְיָ
Eloheinu Melech ha'olam	אֱלֹהֵינוּ מֶלֶךְ הָעוֹלָם
Borei p'ri hagafen	בּוֹרֵא פְּרִי הַגָּפֶן
Amen	אָמֵן

BEFORE EATING CHALLAH:

Baruch Atah Adonai	בָּרוּךְ אַתָּה יְיָ
Eloheinu Melech ha'olam	אֱלֹהֵינוּ מֶלֶךְ הָעוֹלָם
Hamotzi lechem min ha'aretz	הַמּוֹצִיא לֶחֶם מִן הָאָרֶץ
Amen	אָמֵן

BEFORE EATING COOKIES OR SWEETS:

Baruch Atah Adonai	בָּרוּךְ אַתָּה יְיָ
Eloheinu Melech ha'olam	אֱלֹהֵינוּ מֶלֶךְ הָעוֹלָם
Borei minei m'zonot	בּוֹרֵא מִינֵי מְזוֹנוֹת
Amen	אָמֵן

NOTES

www.ingramcontent.com/pod-product-compliance
Lightning Source LLC
Chambersburg PA
CBHW081220230426
43666CB00015B/2826